A Note to Parents and Teachers

Eyewitness Readers is a compelling new reading programme for children. *Eyewitness* has become the most trusted name in illustrated books, and this new series combines the highly visual *Eyewitness* approach with engaging, easy-to-read stories. Each *Eyewitness Reader* is guaranteed to capture a child's interest while developing his or her reading skills, general knowledge and love of reading.

The books are written by leading children's authors and are designed in conjunction with literacy experts, including Cliff Moon M.Ed., Honorary Fellow of the University of Reading. Cliff Moon spent many years as a teacher and teacher educator specializing in reading. He has written more than 140 books for children and teachers, and he reviews regularly for teachers' journals.

The four levels of *Eyewitness Readers* are aimed at different reading abilities, enabling you to choose the books that are exactly right for each child.

Level 1 – Beginning to read
Level 2 – Beginning to read alone
Level 3 – Reading alone
Level 4 – Proficient readers

The "normal" age at which a child begins to read can be anywhere from three to eight years old, so these levels are only general guidelines. No matter which level you select, you can be sure that you're helping children learn to read, then read to

www.dk.com

Editor Dawn Sirett
Art Editor Jane Horne

Senior Editor Linda Esposito
Senior Art Editor
Diane Thistlethwaite
Production Melanie Dowland
Picture Researcher Andrea Sadler
Jacket Designer Margherita Gianni
Natural History Consultant
Theresa Greenaway

Reading Consultant
Cliff Moon, M.Ed.

Published in Great Britain by
Dorling Kindersley Limited
9 Henrietta Street
London WC2E 8PS

2 4 6 8 10 9 7 5 3 1

Eyewitness Readers™ is a trademark of
Dorling Kindersley Limited, London.

Copyright © 1999 Dorling Kindersley Limited, London

All rights reserved. No part of this publication may be
reproduced, stored in a retrieval system, or transmitted
in any form or by any means, electronic, mechanical,
photocopying, recording, or otherwise, without the
prior written permission of the copyright owner.

A CIP catalogue record for this book is
available from the British Library.

ISBN 0-7513-598-66

Colour reproduction by Colourscan, Singapore
Printed and bound in Belgium by Proost

The publisher would like to thank the following for
their kind permission to reproduce their photographs:
Key: t=top, b=bottom, l=left, r=right, c=centre

Colorific: 24 c; **Innerspace Visions:** Marty Snyderman 14 tl; **Frank Lane
Picture Agency:** S. Jonasson 26 br; **London Zoo:** 29 c; **Oxford Scientific
Films:** 26 tr, Alan Root 17 tr; **Planet Earth Pictures:** 5 br, 16 tl; Brian
Kenney 28 bc; **Frank Spooner Pictures:** 24 br; **Tony Stone Images:**
Charley A. Mauzy, Colin Prior front cover background; ©**Barrie
Watts:** 5 t; ©**Jerry Young:** 3 c, 7 bl, 9 cr, 10 tl, 10 br,
13 tr, 15 br, 21 br, 23 c, 25 tl, 25 cr, 32 tl.

Additional credits:
Kenneth Lilly (illustrator); Gary Staab (model maker);
Peter Anderson, Paul Bricknell, Geoff Brightling, Jane Burton,
Gordon Clayton, Geoff Dann, Neil Fletcher, Steve Gorton, Frank
Greenaway, Dave King, Bill Ling, Karl Shone, Steve Shott,
Kim Taylor, David Ward, Jerry Young (photography for DK).

EYEWITNESS READERS

BEGINNING TO READ ALONE 2

Munching, Crunching, Sniffing and Snooping

Written by Brian Moses

DK

London • New York • Sydney • Delhi

Mouths are for eating, drinking and speaking.

Mouths are for tasting, biting and licking.

Mouths are for sipping, chewing and smiling.

Mouths are for singing,
blowing and kissing.

Mouths are for
SHOUTING,
whispering and
YAWNING.

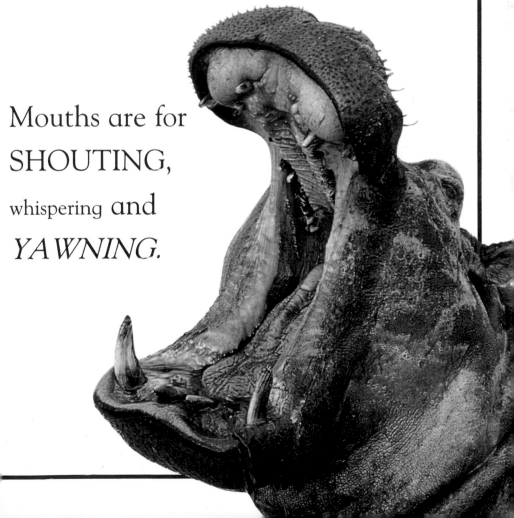

Whose mouths are these?

The king of beasts roams the plain.
He has big, sharp teeth and
a long, shaggy mane.

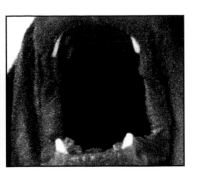

Tell her to sit.
Tell her to lie.
She wags her tail
and jumps up high!

He likes to leap.
He likes to hop.
He dives into ponds.
Splash! Plop! Plop!

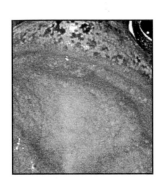

Long and low
with scaly skin,
he lies in water
up to his chin!

Were you right? Turn the page ...

We open our mouths to talk ...

but a lion
roars ...

RRRRr!
RRRRr!

a dog barks ...

WOOF

WOOF

CROAK

a frog croaks ...

and an alligator smiles.
But he's not really smiling.
He's ready to
snap up animals
that come to the river
for a drink.

Body talk

As well as making noises
with their mouths,
many animals "talk"
with their bodies and tails.
This dog wants to play.

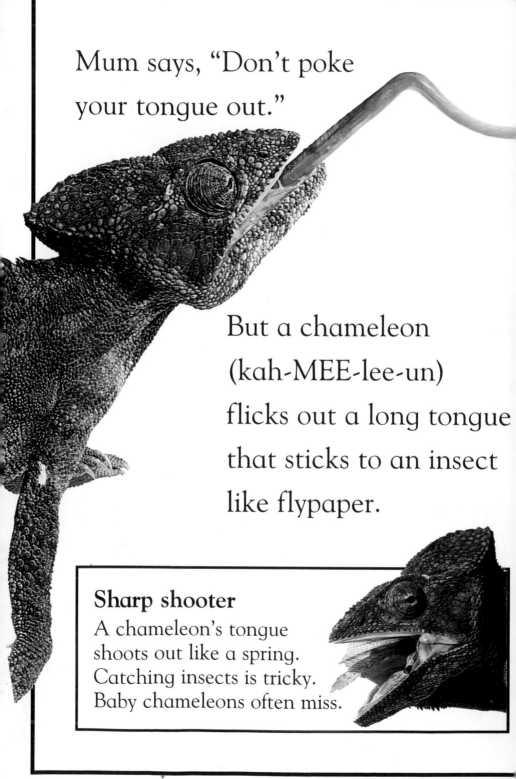

Mum says, "Don't poke your tongue out."

But a chameleon (kah-MEE-lee-un) flicks out a long tongue that sticks to an insect like flypaper.

Sharp shooter
A chameleon's tongue shoots out like a spring. Catching insects is tricky. Baby chameleons often miss.

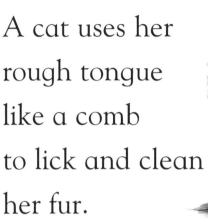

A cat uses her
rough tongue
like a comb
to lick and clean
her fur.

A gecko can clean
his own eyes with
his long tongue.

Dad says, "Don't stand there
with your mouth wide open."

Try telling that to a snake
who is trying to swallow an egg ...

or a howler monkey
who's warning others
not to come
too close ...

or a hyena
who won't
stop laughing.

The hyena's laugh
is no joking matter.
Hyenas make
this sound
when they hunt and
kill their prey.

Mighty biters
Spotted hyenas
have very strong jaws
that can crush and chew
large bones and horns.
Even lions can't do this.

Mum says, "Brush your teeth."

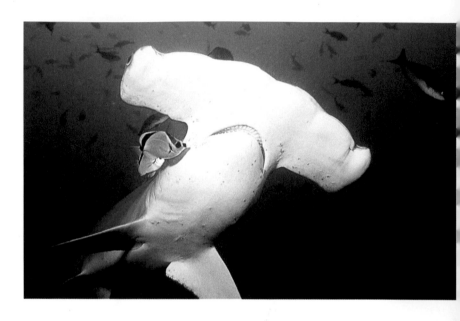

But some sharks
don't need toothbrushes.
Small fish clean their teeth for them

A hamster's strong teeth
never stop growing.
So he doesn't care
about tooth decay.

A turtle never has to worry
about losing her teeth
because she hasn't got any!
Instead, the edges of her jaws
are hard and bony.

Underwater fishing

An alligator snapping turtle's
tongue looks like a worm.
When she opens her mouth,
fish think they see dinner.
They swim in and get snapped up!

A bird's mouth
is called a beak.
Birds use their beak
to collect food and
then eat it.

A heron
has a long,
pointed beak
for catching fish.

A parrot's beak
is so strong
that she can
crack open nuts.

Food on a stick

A woodpecker finch uses his beak to hold a cactus spine which he pushes into tree holes to pick out grubs.

A woodpecker can dig for insects in tree trunks with his sharp beak.

Noses are for smelling,
sniffing and snooping.

Noses are for breathing,
sneezing and snorting.

Noses are for nuzzling up to Mum, for finding food and for staying out of danger.

Noses are for poking ...

but not for picking! Ugh!

Whose noses are these?

In Chinese forests she's top bear.
She's black and white and
very rare.

This animal swings
from tree to tree.
He has fingers and toes
like you and me.

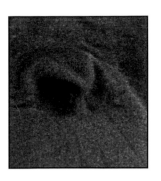

She digs out tunnels
under the ground and
pushes the earth
up into a mound.

He's big and white.
He lives in the snow.
He's covered in fur
from head to toe.

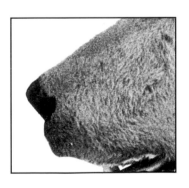

Were you right? Turn the page …

Animals have a much better
sense of smell than we do.
It helps them to find food.

A panda
sniffs out bamboo
which is her
favourite food.

An orangutan
uses his nose
to find the
ripest fruit.

A mole sniffs out earthworms in the dark …

and polar bears sniff out seals that are hiding in the snow.

Sniffing for our supper

People use pigs to sniff out truffles under the ground. Truffles are like mushrooms but they cost a lot more because they are very hard to find.

Mum says, "Don't be nosy."

But police officers never tell their dogs to stop nosing around.

Smelly clues

Police dogs can track down criminals by sniffing small traces of human sweat.

An echidna pokes
his long nose
between rocks,
looking for ants.

Bears stick their noses into beehives
in search of honey.
Their fur protects them
from most bee stings
but sometimes
they get stung
on the nose!

Dad says, "Use a hanky to wipe your nose."

You wouldn't say this to sea birds because they don't carry handkerchiefs ... but they do have runny noses.

Sea birds take in a lot of salt as they feed. Later it comes out through their noses as very salty water.

A camel never has a runny nose.
She can close her nostrils
to keep liquid in and sand out.
This helps her to live
in the hot, dry desert.

Mum says, "If you don't wash, you'll stink."

But some animals stink on purpose.

Skunks can spray a smelly liquid at their enemies. The liquid comes from stink glands under their bushy tails.

Jaguars eat a lot of turtles.

These small animals

are usually easy

to catch.

But this tiny turtle can give off

such an awful smell

that jaguars leave her alone.

No wonder she is called

a stinkpot turtle!

Dad says,
"Don't turn your nose up
at your vegetables."

But you wouldn't
say this to
an elephant.

An elephant's long nose
is called a trunk.
She turns it up to collect leaves to e

She can use it
to lift a log,
suck up water
for a shower,
hold on to another elephant's tail ...
or make a loud noise called trumpeting.

More Fascinating Facts

Female alligators can help their eggs hatch by gently rolling the eggs in their mouths.

When a hippo yawns, he is really warning off other hippos by showing them his huge teeth.

Dogs and cats can carry their young in their mouths without hurting them. They pick up each baby by the scruff of its neck.

A hamster can fill his mouth with lots of food. He stuffs the food in his cheeks, then carries it to his nest, where he stores it for later.

An elephant's trunk can lift a big log but it can also pick up tiny things, such as a single leaf.

A male emperor moth can smell a female several kilometres away.

Salmon are able to smell their way back to the stream where they were hatched.

A snake smells and tastes the air with her tongue. She flicks it in and out to tell whether food, a mate or an enemy is near.